Contents

What is a machine?

A **machine** is anything that helps to make **work** easier. We use machines for almost everything we do. Some are simple, such as scissors. Others are very complicated, such as washing machines.

Scissors are a kind of simple machine that help us to cut. If we didn't have scissors we would have to tear paper with our hands or our teeth.

Science Around Us
Using Machines

Sally Hewitt

Chrysalis Children's Books

First published in the UK in 2003 by
Chrysalis Children's Books
An imprint of Chrysalis Books Group Plc
The Chrysalis Building, Bramley Road
London W10 6SP

Paperback edition first published in 2005
Copyright © Chrysalis Books Group Plc 2003

ISBN 1 84138 719 3 (hb)
ISBN 1 84458 278 7 (pb)

British Library Cataloguing in Publication Data
for this book is available from the British Library.

Editorial manager: Joyce Bentley
Project editor: Clare Weaver
Designer: Wladek Szechter
Picture researcher: Aline Morley
Consultant: Helen Walters

Printed in China

10 9 8 7 6 5 4 3 2 1

Words in **bold** can be found in Words to remember on page 30.

Picture credits
Cover ; Shepard Sherbell/Corbis
Insets (L-R) ; Darama /Corbis, Martin Jackson/Corbis, Lowell Georgia/Corbis, Lowell Georgia/Corbis
Back cover ; Rich Iwasaki/Getty
© Bubbles P4   Loisjoy Thurston, P5 Loisjoy Thurston, P6 Ian West, P8 Loisjoy Thurston, P9 (T) Loisjoy Thurston , P12 Martin Jackson , P16 Pauline Cutler, P17 Loisjoy Thurston, P24 Loisjoy Thurston
© Corbis P7 Robert & Linda Mostyn/ Eye Ubiquitous, P10 Lester Lefkowitz, , P14 Macduff Everton, P15 Tom Stewart, P19 Darama, P21 Lowell Georgia, P23 (T) Museum of Flight, P23 (B) Paul Almasy, P25 Lowell Georgia, P26 Ray Juno, P27 Shepard Sherbell © Getty P1 Rich Iwasaki, P9 (B) Jean Marc-Scialon, P11 John Slater, P13 Christopher Thomas, P18 Ed Pritchard, P20 Rich Iwasaki, P22

A washing machine washes, rinses and spins our dirty laundry. All we have to do is press a button.

Inside a washing machine, water pours through pipes. An electric motor turns the clothes drum.

Without machines things would be much more difficult or take a great deal longer. Imagine how long it would take to wash your clothes without a washing machine.

Machine shapes

Designers make sure machines are the best shape for the **job** they have to do. You can often guess what job a machine does by its shape.

An iron has a flat bottom which is a good shape for pressing out creases and a pointed nose to get into corners.

A strong pointed **metal** rod is a good shape for breaking up the road **surface**.

An iron and a road drill are machines that are held. Their handles are shaped for being held safely and comfortably.

A road drill is a powerful machine for breaking up tough materials like rock and cement.

Machines we use

A car is a machine designed for moving along. The designer must also make sure it is comfortable and **safe** for people to use.

A strong metal body helps to keep the driver and passengers safe.

The driver must be able to see all around her. She needs to reach the **pedals** and the steering wheel easily.

The seat, the mirrors and even the steering wheel can be moved to suit drivers of different sizes.

Normal car seats are too big for the baby. He is safely strapped into his specially designed baby seat.

Wheels

Nearly all machines that move have at least two wheels to roll them along. Enormous trucks have six or more pairs of wheels.

Trucks like these have powerful **engines** to turn their wheels around.

A supermarket trolley has wheels that **swivel**. It can be pushed forwards, backwards and sideways.

Wheels turn around on a rod called an **axle**. A pair of car or truck wheels turn on each end of the axle.

Wheels can be all sizes and made of different **materials,** but they are always round.

cogs

Cogs are wheels with teeth that turn each other round. Cars and bicycles have sets of cog-wheels called **gears** that make them go, speed them up and slow them down.

When you pedal a bike, the pedals turn the chain and cog-wheels, which turn the back wheel around.

The hour, minute and second hands on a clock face are turned around at different speeds by cog-wheels inside a clock.

Winding up a clock tightens a metal **coil** inside. As the coil slowly unwinds it turns the cog-wheels around, which move the hands.

Mountain bike riders can choose from up to 27 different gears to help them speed along flat ground or climb up steep hills.

Levers and hinges

A **lever** is a rod that makes lifting things easier. You pull or push down on one end of a lever to lift a weight at the other end.

The hammer is being used as a lever. Pulling on the hammer pulls the nail out of the wood.

A **hinge** is a kind of lever. It joins two things together and lets them move and bend at the place where they are joined.

Doors open and shut on hinges.

Your elbows and knees work like hinges. They let you bend your arms and legs.

Springs and coils

Springs and coils are both pieces of metal that are wound tightly round and round. A spring bounces up when it is let go and a coil starts to unwind.

A pogo stick has a strong spring that bounces you up and down.

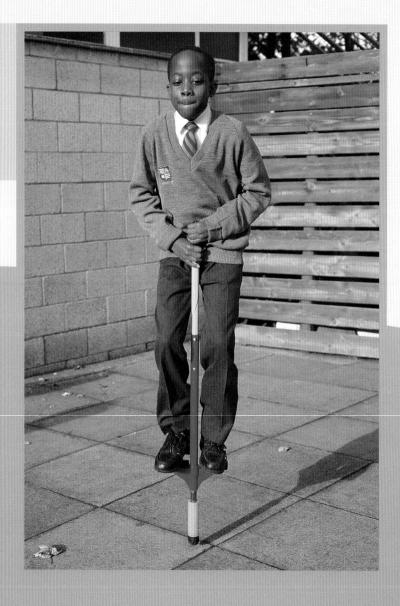

As a coil
unwinds, it moves
things sideways.
A spring moves
things up
and down.

Turning the key of a clockwork toy winds up
a metal coil inside it. As the coil slowly unwinds
it moves other parts of a little machine, which
make the toy move.

Slopes and stairs

Ramps are man-made **slopes**. They are another kind of simple machine that makes lifting things easier. It is easier to push a wheelchair or pushchair up a slope than to lift it up steep steps.

A **conveyor belt** is a machine that makes it easy to move parcels up and down slopes in a factory.

Escalators carry you upstairs and downstairs. All you have to do is stand still.

Stairs and escalators slope upwards.
A lift carries people straight up and down.

An escalator is a moving staircase.
An electric motor inside it turns wheels
around and they move the stairs.

Diggers and cranes

On a building site, diggers break up rocks and dig holes. Cranes lift heavy loads. Wheels, cogs, levers, hinges and pulleys all work together to make these big machines work.

The digger arm is made up of levers that move up and down, backwards and forwards.

A concrete block at one end of the jib stops the crane from tipping over when it is lifting something heavy at the other end.

A pulley is a rope running over wheels. You pull down on the rope to lift up a load.

The lifting arm of a crane is a long lever called a jib. Strong cables run along the jib and over pulley wheels to lift and lower a load.

Trains, boats and planes

Trains, boats and planes are machines that carry us around. They all have powerful engines that drive them along.

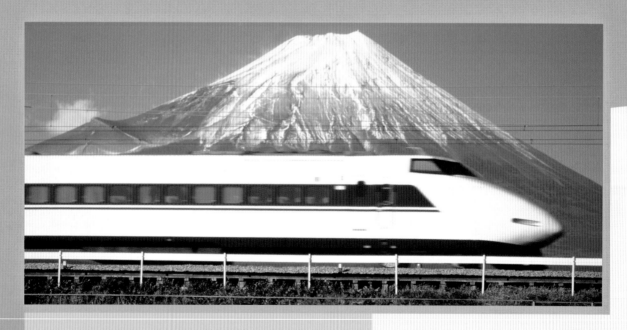

Trains speed along on metal rails. They stop at stations to let passengers on and off.

Planes fly passengers and cargo from place to place. Their engines speed them along the runway. The shape of their wings and tails lifts them off the ground and keeps them flying in the air.

A large jet like this can carry up to 300 passengers.

A hovercraft moves over water. It flies passengers along on a cushion of air.

23

Computers and robots

A computer is a machine with a memory. It can follow instructions and carry out all kinds of different jobs from flying aircraft to weather forecasting.

A click on the mouse tells your computer to send an e-mail to another computer.

A computer is the most complicated machine of all. It is controlled by tiny **microchips** that store billions of bits of information.

A robot called Viking Lander landed on Mars. It carried out orders from Earth and sent back information about the distant planet.

A robot is a kind of computer. It can receive instructions to do a job from miles away.

The car factory

In a car **factory**, machines make the car parts. Workers and robots put the parts together on the assembly line and make a new car ready to drive away.

Computers give instructions to the robot arms to help put the car together.

Not all work
can be done by machines.
Factory workers are
still needed to do
some jobs.

A big car factory can make 1000 cars
in just one day. Imagine how long
it would take to make just one car
without the help of machines.

MAKE A DIGGER

Join three levers together to make a moving digger arm.

YOU WILL NEED:

- strong card
- scissors
- pencil
- ruler
- glue
- 2 paper fasteners
- a hole puncher
- modelling clay

1 Cut a rectangle of card 15 cm by 10 cm for the digger. Punch a hole 1 cm in and halfway down one of the short sides of the digger.

Draw a picture of the driver in his cabin.

2 Cut out three strips of card for the levers.

   Lever 1 6 cm by 2 cm

   Lever 2 7 cm by 2 cm

   Lever 3 8 cm by 2 cm

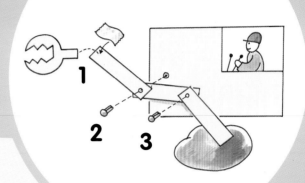

3 Punch a hole in one end of levers 1 and 3.

4 Punch a hole in both ends of lever

5 Join the three levers together with the paper fasteners.

6 Fix paper fastener through the hole in the digger.
Cut out a grab bucket and stick it on the end of lever 1.

7 Push the bottom of the digger into a lump of modelling clay to stand it up.

8 Push and pull lever 3 to move the grab bucket up and down.

Words to remember

axle A rod that goes through the middle of a wheel. A wheel turns around on an axle.

cogs Wheels with teeth that turn each other round. Bicycles and cars have cog-wheels.

coil A strip of metal. A wind-up toy has a coil inside. Turning the key winds the coil tightly round and round.

conveyor belt A machine that makes it easier to move things around, such as boxes in a factory, or luggage at an airport. The belt runs in a loop, carrying things from one place to another.

engine Gives a machine the power to work. A washing machine engine uses electricity and a car engine burns petrol to work.

factory A place where things are made. All the pieces of a car are put together in a car factory.

gear A set of cog-wheels. The gears on a bike change how fast the wheels turn round when you pedal.

hinge A lever that holds two things together. A door hinge holds the door to the door frame and lets it open and shut.

job Work that has to be done. Tidying your bedroom is a job and so is hammering a nail.

lever A simple machine. It is a strong rod used to lift, open and turn.

machine Something that makes work easier. Levers and pulleys are simple machines. An engine is a complicated machine.

materials What things are made of. Wood and wool are natural materials. Plastic is made in a factory.

metal A natural material found in the ground. Iron, steel and gold are different kinds of metal.

microchips Tiny chips made of a material called silicon inside a computer. Each chip stores information and helps to control the computer.

pedals Levers you push with your feet. A car driver pushes pedals to make the car go faster, to slow down and to change gear.

pulley A simple machine. You pull a rope that runs over a pulley wheel to help you to lift up something heavy.

safe To be free from danger.

slope A gently rising hill that makes work easier. It is easier to push or carry something up a slope than to lift it straight up in the air.

spring A strip of metal curled round and round. You can squash a spring. When you let it go, it springs back again.

surface The top or the outside of something. A road surface is usually made of material called tarmac.

swivel To move round and round, in all directions.

work What is done every time something moves, stops, gives out light or heat, or makes a noise. People and machines do work.

Index